US SPECIAL FORCES

DELTA FORCE

By Jeanne Nagle

Gareth Stevens
Publishing

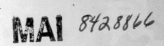

Please visit our website, www.garethstevens.com. For a free color catalog of all our high-quality books, call toll free 1-800-542-2595 or fax 1-877-542-2596.

Library of Congress Cataloging-in-Publication Data

Nagle, Jeanne.
Delta Force / Jeanne Nagle.
    p. cm. — (US Special forces)
Includes index.
ISBN 978-1-4339-6555-5 (pbk.)
ISBN 978-1-4339-6556-2 (6-pack)
ISBN 978-1-4339-6553-1 (library binding)
1. United States. Army. Delta Force—Juvenile literature. 2. United States. Army—Commando troops—Juvenile literature. I. Title.
UA34.S64N47 2012
356'.167—dc23

2011022832

First Edition

Published in 2012 by
Gareth Stevens Publishing
111 East 14th Street, Suite 349
New York, NY 10003

Copyright © 2012 Gareth Stevens Publishing

Designer: Michael J. Flynn
Editor: Kristen Rajczak

Photo credits: Cover, pp. 1, 4–5, 22–23 MILpictures by Tom Weber/The Image Bank/Getty Images; Photos Courtesy of US Army: pp. 6–7 by Lance Cpl. Ronald W. Stauffer, 10–11 by MSG Donald Sparks, SOCEUR Public Affairs, 11 by Amber Avalona-Butler/Paraglide, 12 by Sgt. Ben Watson, 12–13 by Spc. Keith Henning, 14 by Dottie White, 18–19 by Paula M. Fitzgerald/Paraglide, 24–25 by Spc. David Gunn; p. 9 Will McIntyre/Time & Life Pictures/Getty Images; p. 15 (rescue) Alexander Heimann/AFP/Getty Images; p. 15 (inset) David S. Holloway/Getty Images; pp. 16–17 Michel Gangne/AFP/Getty Images; p. 20 Luke Frazza/AFP/Getty Images; pp. 26–27 Archive Photos/Getty Images; p. 28 Manoocher Deghati/AFP/Getty Images; p. 29 Getty Images.

Printed in the United States of America

CPSIA compliance information: Batch #CW12GS: For further information contact Gareth Stevens, New York, New York at 1-800-542-2595.

CONTENTS

WHAT IS DELTA FORCE?

Within the United States military are groups of soldiers who are given the hardest, riskiest **missions**. They are known as Special Forces. They include the Navy SEALs, the Green Berets, and the US Army's 1st Special Forces Operational Detachment, commonly known as Delta Force.

Members of US Special Forces are some of the best-trained soldiers in the world.

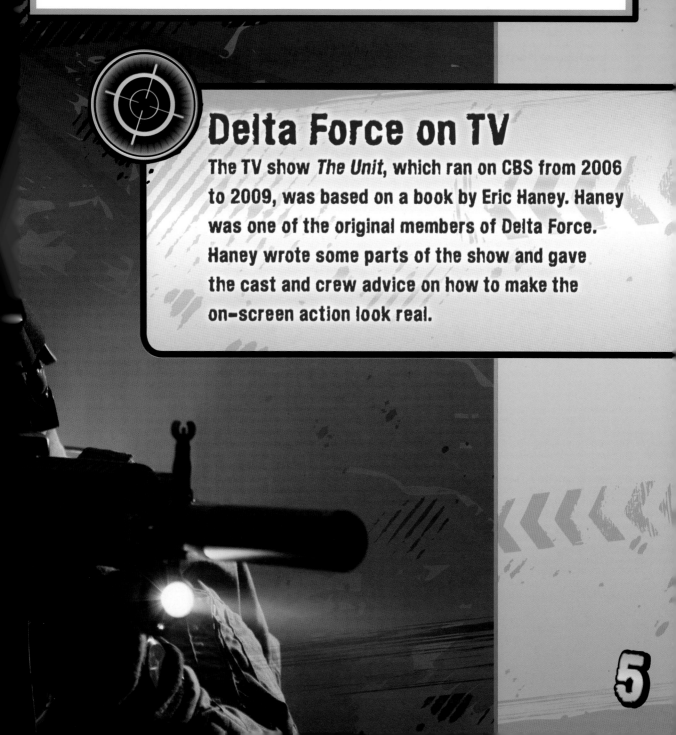

The work Delta Force does is so important that it's often in the news. However, very little is known about this group or its members. All Special Forces, including Delta Force, are covert, which means they operate in secret.

Delta Force on TV

The TV show *The Unit*, which ran on CBS from 2006 to 2009, was based on a book by Eric Haney. Haney was one of the original members of Delta Force. Haney wrote some parts of the show and gave the cast and crew advice on how to make the on-screen action look real.

The members of Delta Force are called operators rather than soldiers. Since this is a covert force, no one knows exactly how many operators there are at any time. It's believed there are 800 to 1,000 active operators. In addition to those who do the actual fighting—called assault forces—there are medical, **intelligence**, training, and other support teams. There's even believed to be a helicopter **platoon**.

Delta Force operators may train to jump from aircraft as well as fly them.

Delta Force operators are organized into at least three and perhaps four **squadrons**. Within each squadron, there are smaller groups called troops. Each troop is composed of teams that specialize in certain skills used in their work, including parachuting, scuba diving, and **sharpshooting**.

Delta Force Women

All the original Delta Force operators were men, and so are most of today's operators. The few women of Delta Force mostly work in the intelligence section, gathering information. The intelligence section is nicknamed the "Funny Platoon."

HOW DELTA FORCE BEGAN

In the 1970s, there was a rise in the number of attacks being committed by **terrorists**. These included **hijacking** planes and killing and kidnapping political figures. The US military saw the need to create a special group whose only job was to fight terrorism. As a result, Delta Force was formed in 1977.

Delta Force's founder, US Army colonel Charles Beckwith, was in charge of picking the first **recruits** from a group of **volunteers**. To make the cut, soldiers had to do dozens of push-ups and sit-ups. Recruits also had to complete long, timed runs while carrying heavy packs.

British SAS

During his military career, Charles Beckwith spent a year working with Britain's Special Air Service (SAS). Formed in 1941 during World War II, the British SAS fights terrorists, rescues **hostages**, and fights enemy troops. Colonel Beckwith patterned Delta Force after the British SAS.

Known as
"Chargin' Charlie,"
Colonel Charles
Beckwith also
worked with the
Green Berets.

9

Today, Special Forces operators like these practice hostage rescue and other missions they may take part in.

Only a few of the early volunteers were chosen to be trained. Many of those who weren't selected either failed the challenging physical tests or felt the pressure was too great and quit before the selection process ended.

After months of training, the original unit's final test is thought to have taken place at a North Carolina location far away from any cities or towns. The men worked as a team to enter both a building and an airplane to rescue pretend hostages. The unit passed this test with flying colors. Delta Force was ready to get to work.

Keep Training!

Constant training allows Delta Force members to keep up to date on the latest **tactics** and weapons. Participating in shared training programs with groups around the world, such as British and Australian SAS units and Israel's Unit 269, also helps Delta Force stay in top fighting form.

These Special Forces operators are training at Fort Bragg in North Carolina.

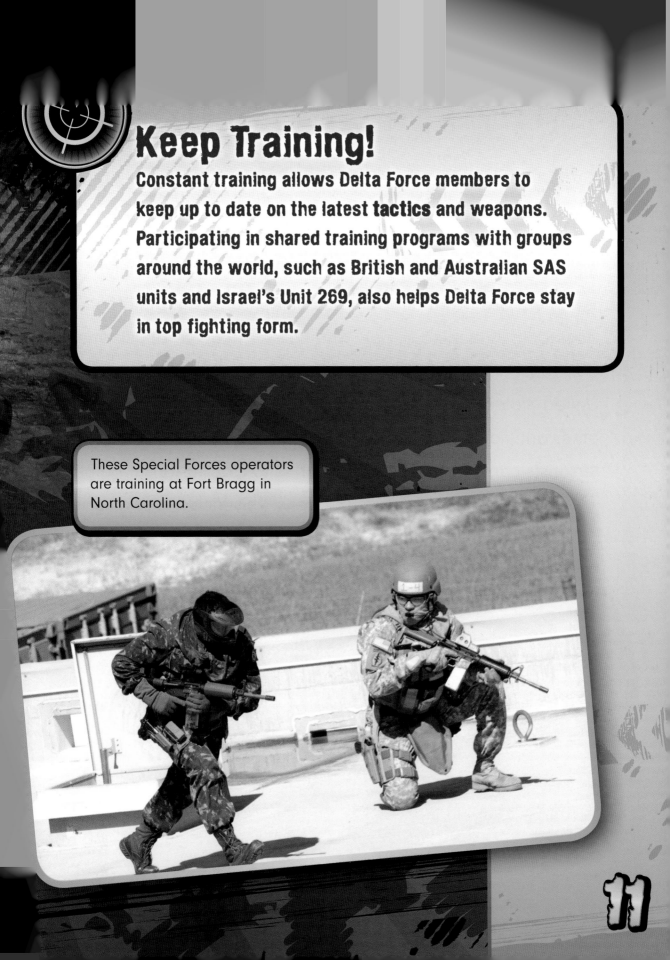

COUNTERTERRORISM

Delta Force's main job today is counterterrorism. This means fighting against and trying to stop terrorist activity.

There are two main parts of counterterrorism. Delta Force does both in the line of duty. The first is to counterattack after a terrorist act occurs. For instance, after the attack against the United States on September 11, 2001, US Special Forces and other arms of the US military attacked the countries where the terrorists came from. The other part is to stop terrorism before it happens. This includes finding the hideouts of people believed to be terrorists and capturing them.

Special Forces operators often work at night in order to stay hidden from enemies.

The black bar added to this picture to cover this man's eyes is meant to hide his face. It's important enemies don't know who Delta Force operators are.

Civilian Missions

As part of the US military, Delta Force isn't supposed to be part of missions involving **civilians** inside the United States. However, the unit helped the FBI stop a 1987 riot in a Georgia prison. In 1993, the unit also set up **surveillance** during a police standoff with a group in Waco, Texas.

HOSTAGE RESCUE

Delta Force operators often rescue people being held hostage. In fact, the unit's first mission was to free Americans being held against their will in Iran in 1980. Since then, the unit has carried out several rescue operations around the world.

Hostage rescue is very hard. Rescuers often have to use force to enter the place where hostages are being held. During the fight, it can be hard to tell who is a hostage and who is a **captor**. Delta Force operators are trained to keep hostages safe while they deal with the captors.

These soldiers are practicing hostage rescue during a US Army contest.

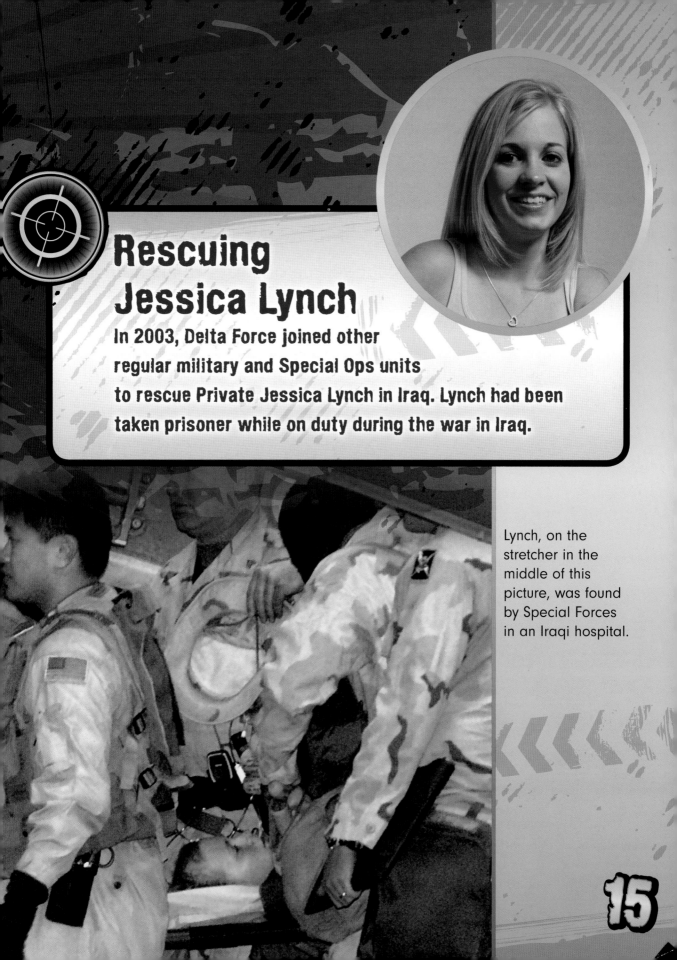

Rescuing Jessica Lynch

In 2003, Delta Force joined other regular military and Special Ops units to rescue Private Jessica Lynch in Iraq. Lynch had been taken prisoner while on duty during the war in Iraq.

Lynch, on the stretcher in the middle of this picture, was found by Special Forces in an Iraqi hospital.

15

SECURITY

Members of Delta Force also do jobs that may not seem as action packed as hostage rescue or secret counterterrorism missions. However, they are just as important. Delta Force is in charge of security in important situations. Operators may protect top US military commanders and leaders visiting from other countries.

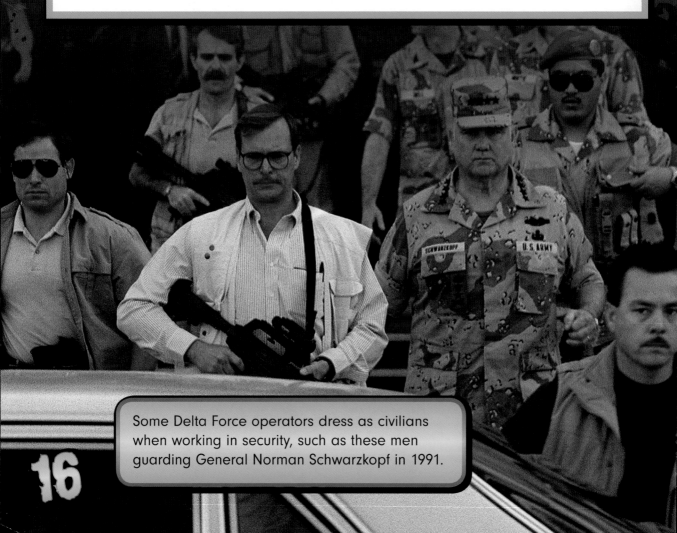

Some Delta Force operators dress as civilians when working in security, such as these men guarding General Norman Schwarzkopf in 1991.

The unit also has provided security for special events with a large international audience. One of the unit's first assignments was to protect players and fans at the 1979 Pan-American Games. Delta Force also has provided security for events such as the Olympic Games in Los Angeles (1984) and Atlanta (1996) and the Statue of Liberty's 100-year celebration in 1986.

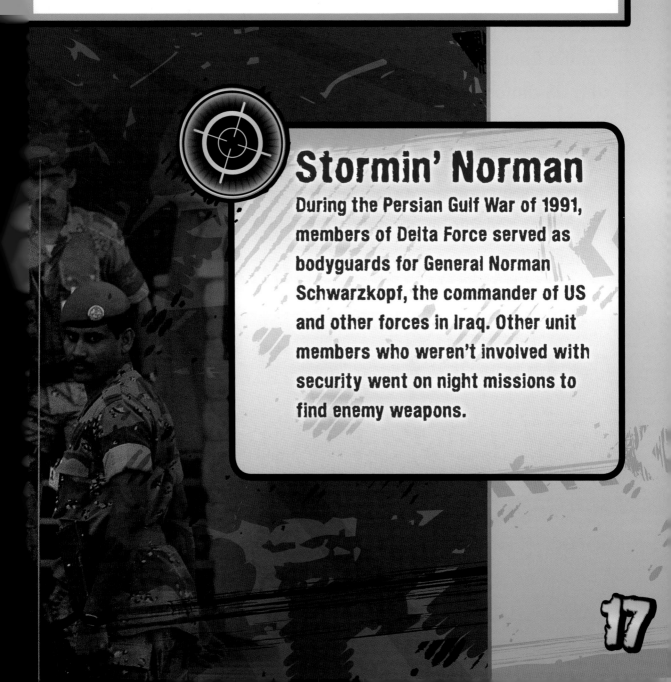

Stormin' Norman

During the Persian Gulf War of 1991, members of Delta Force served as bodyguards for General Norman Schwarzkopf, the commander of US and other forces in Iraq. Other unit members who weren't involved with security went on night missions to find enemy weapons.

RECRUITMENT AND TRAINING

Each year, hundreds of soldiers are recruited for Delta Force or volunteer to become members. A large number of these soldiers come from special units within the US Army, such as the Rangers and the Green Berets. However, any member of the US armed forces can volunteer for Delta Force duty.

In order to be considered for this unit, soldiers must first make it through a selection process. During this time, their skills with guns and other weapons are tested. So are their physical fitness and mental toughness. The selection process lasts an entire month.

Secret Tests

No one knows for sure what qualifications are required for selection to Delta Force. Volunteers must be very good shooters. They have to be able to hit targets 1,000 yards (914 m) away 90 percent of the time. From 600 yards (549 m) away, they must hit the target every time.

Instructors like the man on the right help soldiers prepare for Special Forces training.

President George W. Bush, second from the right, watches Special Forces training in 2002.

20

Soldiers who make it through the tough selection process are allowed to start training to become Delta Force operators. Training takes place at the Fort Bragg military base in North Carolina. Delta Force shares Fort Bragg with other Special Forces units.

The members of Delta Force are trained in many different kinds of skills. For several months, recruits practice target shooting, handling explosives, parachuting out of airplanes, climbing up and down tall buildings, high-speed driving, scuba diving, and hand-to-hand combat. They also receive training in surveillance and other information gathering.

House of Horrors

The "House of Horrors" is a Delta Force training building. Pictures and dummies that look like terrorists and hostages move around its rooms. Recruits learn to shoot with real bullets and often with real people acting as hostages! There's even part of a plane hanging from the ceiling in one part of the building.

WEAPONS AND GEAR

Delta Force operators have many types of weapons and gear available to them. Some of these items are standard issue, meaning everyone in the military has them. An example of a standard-issue weapon is the M-16, a rifle most soldiers carry. Bulletproof vests are worn by all troops fighting on the front lines.

Other weapons are used mainly by Special Ops forces. For instance, lightweight machine guns and **grenade** launchers that can be attached to rifles are often used. Delta Force operators also often have guns specially made for them.

Flash-Bang

During rescue operations, Delta Force uses a special type of grenade called the "flash-bang." The grenade's very loud noise and bright light briefly deafen and blind terrorists, making it easier for operators to get in and save hostages.

These Special Forces operators carry the rifles troops use in Afghanistan.

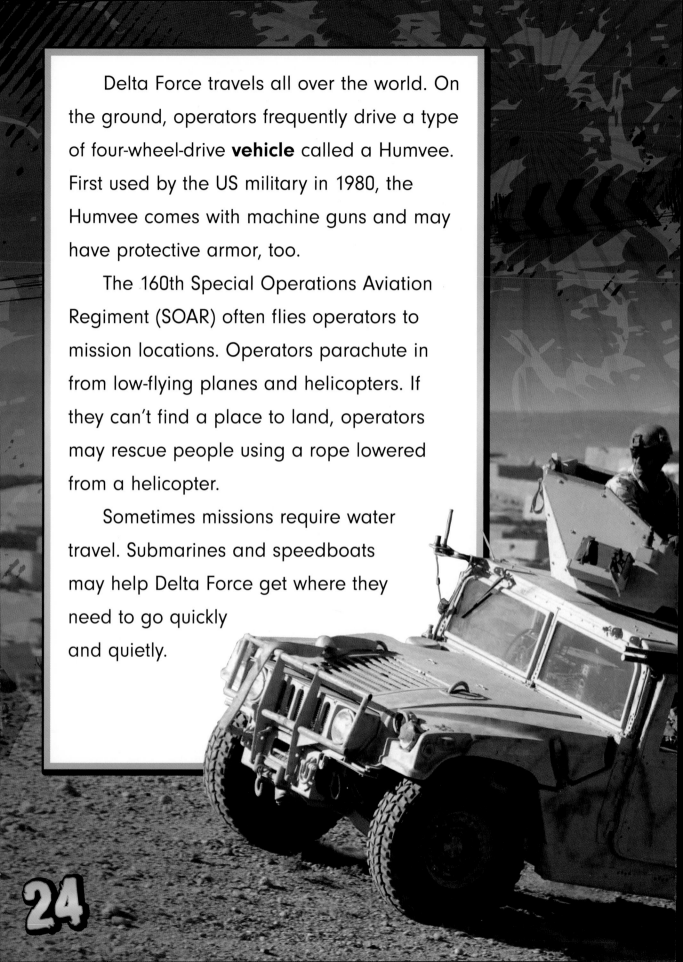

Delta Force travels all over the world. On the ground, operators frequently drive a type of four-wheel-drive **vehicle** called a Humvee. First used by the US military in 1980, the Humvee comes with machine guns and may have protective armor, too.

The 160th Special Operations Aviation Regiment (SOAR) often flies operators to mission locations. Operators parachute in from low-flying planes and helicopters. If they can't find a place to land, operators may rescue people using a rope lowered from a helicopter.

Sometimes missions require water travel. Submarines and speedboats may help Delta Force get where they need to go quickly and quietly.

FAVs

Fast Attack Vehicles (FAVs), now called Desert Patrol Vehicles (DPVs), were lightly armored dune buggies. They were easy to drive in the sand. Delta Force and the Navy SEALs used FAVs for desert fighting during wars in the Persian Gulf. Other units in the US military now use similar vehicles called Light Strike Vehicles (LSVs).

A group of Special Forces operators drive a Ground Mobility Vehicle in Afghanistan.

FAMOUS OPERATIONS

Delta Force has worked on many missions, or operations. The following are some of the most famous operations in the unit's history. Each is listed by year and code name.

1980 – Operation Eagle Claw

Operation Eagle Claw was an attempt to rescue hostages in Iran. Unfortunately, it didn't go well. A helicopter and plane crashed and burned before the hostages could be rescued.

1983 – Operation Urgent Fury

Delta Force was part of the US military action on the island nation of Grenada. Operators tried to set political prisoners free from a prison named Richmond Hill.

Political Prisoners

Political prisoners are people who are put in jail for their beliefs. Usually, they're held prisoner because they don't support the government in power. Delta Force may be sent to other countries to rescue political prisoners whose lives are in danger.

US troops open fire during Operation Urgent Fury in Grenada.

1989 – Operation Just Cause

General Manuel Noriega became a military **dictator** in Panama. He was in the drug trade, so the US government wanted him out of power. Delta Force helped find him and also rescued a US citizen who was being held prisoner during this time.

1993 – Operation Restore Hope

This mission began as a way to get food to starving people in Somalia. Later, Delta Force and other military groups tried to capture Mohamad Farah Aidid, the leader who was responsible for the starvation.

1998 – Operation Allied Force

Members of Delta Force were sent to Kosovo to collect intelligence and help the military there.

Modern Operations

In 2003, Delta Force hunted for and captured Saddam Hussein, the dictator in Iraq who was believed to be connected to terrorists. Some people think that Delta Force also helped the Navy SEALs find the terrorist Osama bin Laden in 2011.

US soldiers celebrate the finding of Saddam Hussein in 2003.

GLOSSARY

captor: someone who holds another person prisoner

civilian: a person not on active military duty

dictator: a leader who has total power and often limits citizens' rights

grenade: a small bomb thrown by hand or by a launcher

hijack: to take control of a vehicle by force

hostage: someone who is being held against his or her will

intelligence: in the military, gathering information about a possible enemy

mission: a task

platoon: a small group of soldiers who work together

recruit: a new member of a military force

sharpshooting: shooting with great skill and few errors

squadron: a division of military organization, smaller than a unit but larger than a platoon

surveillance: the act of watching someone or something closely

tactic: a method for accomplishing a military goal

terrorist: one who uses violence and fear to challenge an authority

vehicle: an object used for carrying or transporting people or goods, such as a car, truck, or airplane

volunteer: a person who offers to do something

FOR MORE INFORMATION

Books

Burnett, Betty. *Delta Force: Counterterrorism Unit of the U.S. Army.* New York, NY: Rosen Central, 2003.

Hamilton, John. *Special Forces.* Edina, MN: ABDO Publishing Company, 2007.

Riley, Gail Blasser. *Delta Force in Action.* New York, NY: Bearport Publishing, 2008.

Websites

Elite UK Forces: Special Air Service
www.eliteukforces.info/special-air-service/
Find out about the unit that inspired the creation of Delta Force.

Office of the Coordinator for Counterterrorism
www.state.gov/s/ct/
Read more about the government office in charge of counterterrorism.

US Army Special Forces
www.goarmy.com/special-forces.html
Learn more about the Special Forces and how soldiers become a part of them.

INDEX